Dancing Alone

Cover & title page art: Chris Wells © 2004
Author photograph by John Garner
Design and in-house editing by Joe Blades.
Printed and bound in Canada by Sentinel Printing, Yarmouth NS.

cauldron books

A book series edited by Ottawa writer/editor/publisher rob mclennan. Named after the Celtic idea of the cauldron as the keeper & dispenser of wisdom & knowledge. The series will focus not only on worthwhile collections of poetry, but on single author collections of essays, as writing on writing. The cauldron books series is published by Broken Jaw Press. rob may be found on the web at www.track0.com/rob_mclennan and reached via email at <az421@freenet.carleton.ca>, www.brokenjaw.com/cauldronbooks.htm

Broken Jaw Press acknowledges the support of the Canada Council for the Arts and the New Brunswick Culture and Sport Secretariat-Arts Development Branch.

Broken Jaw Press Inc. **www.brokenjaw.com**
Box 596 Stn A
Fredericton NB E3B 5A6
Canada

Library and Archives Canada Cataloguing in Publication

Hawkins, William, 1940-
Dancing alone : selected poems / William Hawkins.

(Cauldron books ; 5)
Includes bibliographical references.
ISBN 1-55391-034-6

I. Title. II. Series.

PS8515.A895D36 2005 C811'.54 C2005-901684-1

DANCING ALONE

Selected Poems

WILLIAM HAWKINS

cauldron books 5

Fredericton • Canada

for my mother, always...

DANCING ALONE

Preface, by Bruce Cockburn ... 9

William Hawkins: A Unique Voice in Canadian Poetry,
by Roy MacSkimming ... 11

Sunrise ... 21
King Kong Goes to Rotterdam ... 22
Postage Stamps ... 23
Two Short Ones ... 24
The Vision of King Mountain ... 25
Xochiquetzal ... 26
King Kong Goes to Saudi-Arabia ... 27
A Song of Flowers ... 28
Porsche ... 29
For Jenny Louisa Lockyear ... 30
Birth ... 31
Billy Graham Goes to Tallahassee ... 32
Woman from Tallahassee ... 33
A Monster's Travelogue ... 34
What He's Waiting For ... 35
The Only Flag ... 36
November 17, 1963 ... 37
Put Down ... 38
Maidanek ... 39
Four Songs of Experience ... 40
A New Light ... 43
Letter ... 44
Spring Rain ... 45
For David Wiffen ... 46
Impressions of a Mythical Being ... 47
Youth ... 51
The Wall ... 52
Schoenberg ... 53
The Seed ... 54
Pounding on the Front Door, Coming in the Back ... 55

Mysteriensonaten 56
Fragment of a Conversation 57
Louis Riel 58
from *Ottawa Poems* 77
#1 77
#2 78
#3, The Funny Kind of Prophet Speaks 79
#4 80
#5 81
#6 82
#7, A Mild Effort at Philosophy 83
#10 84
#11 85
#12 86
#14 87
#15, Ah shit don't shoot I'll sing 88
#16 90
#17 91
#18 92
#19, Homage to Batman 93
#21 94
#22, You In The Morning 95
#23, Hello from the Shadows 96
#25, The Last Train to Narcissus 97
#27 99
Books on Iran Wanted 99
The Stupid Saint 102
Wilful Murder 103
Wystan Hugh Auden 104
A Gift for Caesar 105
Angel of Death in My Dreams 106
A Poem About Tomorrow 107
Before She Could Do It 108
A Powerful Cat 109
Paper Roses 110
The Gift of Space 111
The Warner Mystique 112
Projective Tulips 113

Expanded Translation of a Half-Remembered Haiku 114
The High-Flying Eagle 115
Peg's Dream 116
Autistic 117
A Delineation of Memories 118
Invocation 122
Weather Report 123
Stormcentre: Cassandra 124
Cassandra's Communication Network 125
Cassandra on a Bender 126
Cassandra's Explicit Sacrament 127
On His Thirtieth Year 128
Bar La Cueva 129
Tequila Puro 130
Another Day in the Bar La Cueva 131
The Ghost of a Rooster Killed by Ritual 132
King Billy, the Disenchanted 133
Recollection of Celebration 134
October 1st 1968 135
Male/fail Tale 136
Mexican Ice Cream Master 137
Cerveza Superior 138
A Walk in A Certain Plaza 139
A Blue Bell 140
Poopsie/Power/Poem 141
Batting Practice 142
Forslack and Forless 143
Rhyme Suggestion 144
When I Fall In Love 145
Intimations of Amorality 146
The Madman's War 147
The Madman's War: the winter offensive 1973/74 148
Declaration of Dependence 149
Suicide Note 150
O Carole 151
Scarlet Woman With Blue Angora Scarf 152
Untitled Fragment 153
Sacrifice 154

How the Dead Prey Upon You 155
Small Ankles, Take Two 156
Dim Aspirations 157
Turning Things Around 158
Switching Lanes 159
Sheila Frances Louise 160
Sunrise: Villanelle 161

Acknowledgements 163

About the Author 165

Preface

When i started writing songs, it was to put music to Bill Hawkins' lyrics. I'd met him a couple of years earlier, when he was managing Le Hibou, a coffee house in Ottawa, which was where i first performed in public as myself. I'd been fascinated by the power of poetic language since public school, and to meet a "real" poet was very exciting. I was in high school. Not much else in my life was even interesting. Primed by readings of Beat literature, i quickly fell under the spell of this charismatic man who became a kind of mentor. I'm sure Bill would have recoiled from the idea had he known that's how i saw him, but something in the chemistry between our two damaged selves worked for him, too.

At the end of 1965 i dropped out of music school and joined The Children, a band of friends committed to performing an eclectic range of original material. Hawkins was the creative catalyst—the brains of the gang—lurking in the background rather than performing with us (except when we opened for The Lovin' Spoonful at Maple Leaf Gardens and Bill sat on stage in a rocking chair and read while we played).

I lived with the Hawkins family for something like a year, during which time Bill introduced me to the poetry of Olson, Rimbaud, Cendrars and so much more; to profound spiritual concepts embodied in the Tarot and other occult disciplines. Watching him work his own word magic taught me a lot. He encouraged me to try and write my own song lyrics. I guess it took.

I'm glad an opportunity has come to publicly thank him for his contribution to my life.

Bill, thanks—for tolerance, for advice, for observations made and doors opened.

Everyone should read these poems.

Bruce Cockburn OC
August 2004

William Hawkins: A Unique Voice in Canadian Poetry

It was poesy, as we mockingly called it, that brought Hawkins and me together. The year was 1962. We were an unlikely pair. Not long before, I'd been playing fullback for my Ottawa high school, trying for straight A's and a university scholarship. Bill had been doing time in Quebec's Val Tetreau correctional institution for some misdemeanor involving other people's cars. He had the tattoo to prove it—a pattern of five bluish-black dots on the back of his left hand, the mark by which alumni of the prison system recognized each other.

By then, Bill's felonious past was more or less past. But in my naïve, romantic, middle-class view, he still lived dangerously. He took drugs, drank too much, insulted important people. In fact he insulted most people, important or not, more or less on principle. A few exceptions earned his respect—artists of one kind or another, who were his close friends. Somehow I became one of those. I was flattered. I was eighteen, and Bill at twenty-two was the nearest thing Ottawa had to an authentic contemporary poet: the genuine article.

In Bill's early poetry, you could detect his influences—Blake and Whitman, Irving Layton, and, most strikingly, the Beat bop prosody of Allen Ginsberg and Gregory Corso. But Hawkins was no slavish imitator waiting for his adult identity to arrive. He was precocious in already laying claim to a distinctive voice and vision. His rhetoric was extravagantly theatrical, with a dark disturbing undertow never far from the surface. Just listen to this remarkable line from "A Monster's Travelogue," one of his delightfully bizarre King Kong poems:

Battered & ball-wracked, immense pilgrim snug in his cups of horror

In life too, Bill was an original, at least in Ottawa terms. His publishing method, for example. I was taking the conventional route, mailing my poems off to little literary mags like *Evidence*, *The Fiddlehead*, *Canadian Forum*. Although I had some success, Bill was doing something edgier and more enterprising. He collaborated with other local artists—the painters Andries Hamann and Christopher Wells, the printer-printmakers Robert

Rosewarne and Fran Jones—to create poster poems: arresting visual settings of his poetry in linocut, printed on big sheets and sold for beer money, or simply posted around town in busy public places. These artifacts were artworks in themselves. They were also bold statements about taking poetry out of the libraries and lecture halls and sticking it in the public square, right in people's faces. As a measure of the distance society has travelled since then, particularly in the staid capital city, taking poetry to the people was an insolent, radical, unheard-of act. I was captivated.

To enter Bill's circle was to discover, amazedly, that Ottawa had its own bohemian underground. The hub was Le Hibou, a coffee house managed in the early days by Hawkins himself. Later Le Hibou would relocate to grander, street-level quarters in a heritage building on Sussex, but in '62 it was a small, dark, narrow *boîte* in a Bank Street walkup near Laurier, where folksingers and poets appeared on a tiny stage in front of tables holding candles stuck into Chianti bottles.

That little candlelit room gave local musicians their start and once played host to an all-star poetry series, featuring readings by Layton, Louis Dudek, Raymond Souster, Gwendolyn MacEwen, John Robert Colombo and Peter Miller. Hawkins, aided and abetted by his wife Sheila Hawkins, opened and closed the place every evening, ran the kitchen, introduced the acts, and looked after visiting musicians of the likes of young Gordon Lightfoot, Mark Spoelstra and Ramblin' Jack Elliott, which usually involved putting them up on his living room couch. Bill's biggest challenge in the job was the necessity to curb his tongue a little. It almost mellowed him.

In summer 1963, when I returned home from my first year at the University of Toronto, Bill badly needed a break from Le Hibou and the confines of the hometown. By now he and Sheila had two children. He became enormously excited about a summer writing course being offered by the University of British Columbia English department: an intensive program for aspiring poets, who would be juried into the program on the quality of their work. The program offered the chance to work with an absolutely astonishing "faculty" including Allen Ginsberg, Charles Olson, Robert Duncan and the program's organizer, Robert Creeley. Sheila was willing—who knows, maybe eager—to let Bill go. All he lacked was money and transportation.

Persuading me to go with him solved the latter problem, since I owned a sort of car—a quaint, arthritic Morris Minor convertible, a model now prized by connoisseurs. To scrounge the necessary cash, Bill decided to stage a fundraiser at Le Hibou under the rubric "Help Get Hawkins Out of Town." It featured, in addition to Bill and me reading from our work, performances by a bluegrass duo calling itself Peter and Nev (Peter Hodgson, later renamed Sneezy Waters, and Neville Wells, both of whom would become country singers) and a shy, solemn eighteen-year-old guitarist named Bruce Cockburn, who played some Spanish classical pieces rather beautifully.

Fortunately the UBC program accepted us both. The Morris Minor broke down beside the Blackfoot reserve at Gleichen, Alberta and barely made it over the Rockies. But once in Vancouver after sleeping in a tent every night, Bill and I had a variety of life-changing experiences. For a month we hung out day and night, in classrooms and readings and parties, with other young poets, mainly from the west, some of them terrific—among them George Bowering, Lionel Kearns, Fred Wah, Jamie Reid, Robert Hogg, David Cull, and Dan McLeod, future publisher of *The Georgia Straight.*

But it was the faculty, in reality exemplars and inspirations, who remain most vivid in memory. Ginsberg was a sweet-souled miracle. To lounge in a group with him on the campus grass was to glimpse the possibility of serenity. Olson was a powerful intellectual presence, whose poetry I found overly cerebral but whose monologues on history and poetics were riveting. Duncan read his own long poems like an angel. But he who engaged us most deeply, through his work as well as his personality, conversation and readings, was Bob Creeley—a lovely man full of self-doubts and honest hesitations and humorously generous impulses. For Bill, especially, Creeley's artistic impact was profound. Creeley's short, rue-filled lines measured to his breath patterns flooded Bill's cortex in ways that would change his poetry for good. It was too synchronistic for words that, when the Morris collapsed again on our return trip through East Wenatchee, Washington, Creeley materialized over breakfast in a Chinese café and paid the mechanic's bill we couldn't afford.

After our transcontinental adventure, Bill entered a prolific creative period. Over the next seven years, '64 to '71, he'd publish five collections of poetry, appear in two landmark anthologies, and start to become recognized nationally. He'd also have a major impact on the Ottawa music scene as a singer-songwriter and instigator of adventurous new bands. And at the end of that period, like Rimbaud, whom he resembled in more ways than one, he'd more or less give it all up—not announcing it or anything, just wandering off and subsiding into other obsessions.

Bill's first two books were self-published collaborations quite different in style and substance. With me he put out *Shoot Low Sheriff, They're Riding Shetland Ponies* (no publisher stated, 1964), a 56-page stapled paperback with droll cover portraits of the two of us by Chris Wells. Half the work is mine, the other half Bill's: a striking group of 23 poems, mostly from his Beat, pre-Vancouver period—all the King Kong poems are there—but also a few later pieces starting to show his transition to shorter lines, less florid rhetoric and more personal themes. Bill and I peddled *Shoot Low* for a dollar to bookstores in Ottawa and Toronto until our friend Bill Roberts of Shirley Leishman Books, for whom Bill later worked, took over distribution. At last report, a few remaining copies of this modest volume are available at lavish prices from rare book dealers.

Bill's second collaboration was with another Ottawa poet living in Toronto, Harry Howith. *Two Longer Poems* (Patrician Press, Toronto, 1965) consists of Howith's *The Seasons of Miss Nicky* and Hawkins' *Louis Riel.* Moved by George F.G. Stanley's biography of Riel, Bill identified intensely (I believe) with the doomed Métis leader and wrote a 36-page sequence of meditations on Riel's visions, madness (the poem's term) and execution. Although it doesn't finally succeed, to my mind, as art, the poem contains brilliant flashes of insight and imagery and stands as a rare and gutsy example of applying Pound's and Olson's poetics to Canadian history.

The year 1966 was Bill's *annus mirabilis.* Within twelve months he produced his two finest individual collections and appeared alongside some of the best young poets of his generation in Ray Souster's classic anthology, *New Wave Canada.*

At 52 pages, *Hawkins* (Nil Press, Ottawa, 1966) collected Bill's short poems from the previous three years, post-Vancouver. Cleverly designed by Bob Rosewarne at his Nil Press, the poems looking raw in typewriter font as if yanked straight from the manuscript, the book again received distribution through Leishman's.

The Ottawa Poems was in fact published elsewhere (Weed/flower Press, Kitchener, 1966), by the poet, publisher and antiquarian book dealer

Nelson Ball. These poems are ruminations on identity and meaning in the context of a life in

This crazy river-abounding town
where people are quietly
following some hesitant
form of evolution
arranged on television
from Toronto.

Because they belong to a loosely linked sequence, these are more abstracted and discursive poems than the tighter, imagistic, self-contained pieces in *Hawkins*. And perhaps because they often look outward to the surrounding society, they're also more anxious and fearful, occasionally a touch paranoid:

I sing:
Ottawa,
rivers & jails,
fantasies
the dawn can't
slow up.

When Ray Souster was deciding which poets to include in *New Wave Canada: The New Explosion in Canadian Poetry* (Contact Press, Toronto, 1966), he relied for suggestions on Victor Coleman, the poet and editor at Coach House Press. Coleman hadn't attended the UBC poetry program, but many of his fellow-travellers in Black Mountain poetics had; the anthology included Cull, Hogg, Reid and Wah, as well as Hawkins and MacSkimming. Others among the seventeen contributors were Daphne Buckle (later Marlatt), George Jonas, Barry Lord, bp Nichol, David McFadden, Michael Ondaatje and Coleman himself.

For Bill, appearing in Souster's anthology helped give his work national recognition and provided an unexpected consequence. The establishment critic A.J.M. Smith was assembling an anthology for Oxford University Press of outstanding Canadian poetry since the rise of modernism in the 1920s. Smith happened upon the page proofs of *New Wave Canada* (Coleman was working at Oxford at the time), and Hawkins was one of four poets from the Contact Press book who caught Smith's eye. Three poems of Bill's duly appeared in *Modern Canadian Verse* (OUP, Toronto, 1967), tucked between work by Margaret Atwood and Gwen MacEwen.

This was heady recognition for a twenty-seven-year-old graduate of Val Tetreau. But Bill was already veering away from poesy toward another, parallel career. Folk and pop music were both passing through incredibly fertile periods. Bob Dylan, John Lennon, Gordon Lightfoot and Joni Mitchell were poets in their own right. Bill's sometime friend and fellow acid-tripper Leonard Cohen was taking the opposite route, from literature into music. Bill did likewise.

Hanging out with musicians at the relocated Le Hibou, he got to know not only visiting stars like Cohen, Judy Collins, John Hammond and Tim Hardin, but locally based talents such as Bruce Cockburn, David Wiffen, Colleen Peterson, Amos Garrett and Darius Brubeck, son of Dave. Bill started putting bands together. His force of personality, worldliness and relative maturity made him a natural leader. Just as importantly, he was writing plenty of strong original material for his musicians to play and sing. And always Harvey Glatt, then owner of Treble Clef record stores and concert presentations, and later founder and principal owner of CHEZ-FM, was there in the background, advising them on artistic, legal and financial matters, investing in their talent, giving them a chance. Harvey was, and remains, a quietly influential animator of Ottawa's artistic life, an entrepreneur with soul. He was always a supporter of Bill's peculiar genius.

The personnel in Bill's bands constantly shifted and reformed, according to circumstance and the vagaries of who happened to be in town. They were called The Children (with a nucleus of Cockburn, Wiffen, Neville Wells, Sneezy Waters, Sandy Crawley and Richard Patterson) and Heavenly Blue (after the morning glory seeds that get you high)—and once, on the occasion of the Queen's Centennial visit to Ottawa, The Occasional Flash, playing before Her Majesty at Lansdowne Park. They performed Bill's music for Pierre Elliott Trudeau's victory party in 1968 and for the National Film Board release *Christopher's Movie Matinee*. Bill's songs began to get around. They were recorded by Tom Rush, Brent Titcomb, Three's A Crowd (Wiffen, Titcomb and Donna Warner) and The Esquires. "It's a Dirty Shame" in The Esquires' version hit number one regionally. When Bill went on a reading tour with Irving Layton to Toronto's Global Village, the National Arts Centre and elsewhere, he read a few poems but spent most of his time onstage singing his songs, accompanying himself (badly) on the guitar.

Somewhere in there, Bill was selected one of "Ottawa's Outstanding Young Men" along with the developer Bill Teron and the Rough Riders' star quarterback Russ Jackson. (Bill was presented with a plaque, which he used for cutting hash.) Eventually Cockburn, after releasing his first couple of solo albums, told *Maclean's* it was Hawkins who had shown him how to write songs.

By then it was the early '70s. The '60s, with their endless license and love affair with the improvised inspiration, were giving way to a more ordered approach to life. I'd been a publisher's editor in Toronto for several years and was working as a partner at a small press when we decided to publish Bill's selected poems. *The Gift of Space: Selected Poems 1960/70* (New Press, Toronto, 1971) is a hardcover, unpaginated, with another great cover drawing by Chris Wells: Bill being transported atop King Kong's brawny shoulders. *The Gift of Space* drew on what I considered Bill's best work from *Shoot Low, They're Riding Shetland Ponies*; *Hawkins*; and *The Ottawa Poems*. Until now, it's been the only substantial, representative sampling of his work.

Bill published only one more collection after that: a slim volume (32 pages) of new work called *The Madman's War* (S.A.W. Publications, Ottawa, 1974). Many of those poems had been written during a trip to Mexico with Sheila and the children in 1968; others were written later, after their marriage breakup. In its spirit of exhaustion and futility, the work is reminiscent of Malcolm Lowry in *Under the Volcano*. The front cover photo shows a very long-haired Bill cradling a rifle, the back cover photo suggests serious war damage—Bill looking wiped out, with a bandage wrapped around his head—and the last poem in the book is titled "Suicide Note."

Although Bill's private wars took their toll on his body and his writing, he's a survivor. Thankfully, he's still with us: a well-known Ottawa figure behind the wheel of his big Blue Line cab, transporting judges and MPs and journalists to their assignations, chatting knowledgeably all the way about politics, literature and life. His work is still with us too, thanks to this volume from publisher Joe Blades of Broken Jaw Press in Fredericton and his Ottawa-based poetry editor, rob mclennan.

The poems in this book are undeniable evidence that here is a distinctive, inimitable voice in Canadian poetry. Taken together, Hawkins' work is almost unbearably poignant in its existentialism verging on nihilism. It expresses a felt beauty and innocence that must remain unattainable, insisting on the ultimate certainty of loss, emptiness, death. Yet somehow the poet can't help betraying a mordant love of the whole ironic process. Although his poems often appear casual, constructed of throwaway lines and impromptu endings, the best of them are spare, stark, unadorned gestures, brought off as swiftly and unerringly as a Zen painting. They can take your breath away—a quality that no doubt struck A.J.M. Smith when he chose a poem like "Spring Rain" for his Oxford anthology:

SPRING RAIN

This black life
this conversing with shadows

& what about reality
or economic aspects, restricting movement,
halting growth
or the children in a room apart
torturing themselves?

are we not mutations
reconciling diverse things?

is not water
a symbol of life
& this life of death?

is not that haze
before my eyes
spring rain?

This very welcome volume gives a new generation, and those who missed it the first time around, an opportunity to discover William Hawkins' poetry in all its perversely compelling, idiosyncratic wonder.

Roy MacSkimming
Perth, Ontario
June 2004

DANCING ALONE

Selected Poems

WILLIAM HAWKINS

Sunrise
(for Carl Andries Hamann)

Day break me a day of no regret
Regret is the name of the days I get
Day break me this day for I've not lived yet
                    Cuz
                      O
                  I would bring
        lollipops to all bad sad boys and girls
        and would make the livid churches run
        leap frog! leap frog! leap frog!

If you
Sun
  would just break regretless
  with a sunrise of elephant parades
I could bring an end to the reign of trees that bleed
Day break me a day of no regret
Day break me this day for I've not lived yet
Sunrise of elephant parades.

King Kong Goes to Rotterdam

Why now King Kong me
Me silent seeker of the Rotterdam of pussycats
Me troubled watcher of St. Orlovsky's bear
I'm in the ice-bags of tomorrow's girl
My endless aspirations of Holland won't save me
I've seen the blond girls of Rotterdam copulating
Oblivious of world sorrow
But ecstatic for corduroy trousers

I wear corduroy trousers
Yet I am a billion miles from pigtails

Postage Stamps

Now in my twenty-first year
brick vaults
function against me
O loomtazark and blip-foo
I think it's the end
people
and I must say something
or do something
So I run thru it all
down the Mall
and Bank Street too
my head covered
with postage stamps
crying
mail me!
mail me!
And the crazy people ask
and where
Billy
and where
And I say
O anywhere

Two Short Ones

I am told that pigeons
or birds of some sort
shit all over Beethoven's statue
in Vienna
I used to like birds
now
I just don't know
what to think

... ...

My friend Hamann is painting the end of it all
It's all square to him
and I don't understand
I tell him
in an elaborate manner
that I don't understand
and he is elated
My friend Hamann also likes birds
and me and Ludwig
find that hard to take

The Vision of King Mountain

Surrounded by the myth of big men
And the reality of girl-boys
                                        I
                              neither big man nor girl-boy
Stand alone in these Autumn-exhausted hills
Praying for rabbits
                            hating the cold
                  and wishing that the obvious vision of King Mountain
                      would reveal itself to me

And yet I am unable to climb to the peak of that mountain
Where all visions are possible
I stay over the automobile-slain body of a rabbit
Trying to draw an insane line of relation
From the big men to the girl-boys to the dead rabbit

I am a child of Autumn
See the orange in my eyes

Xochiquetzal

A flower saddened by the grief of years,
Zoned by trees, impaled on three-pronged Spanish spears,
To you, Xochiquetzal, my marriage song is sung,
Epithalamium for a much suffered and suffering one
Caught and bald-headed with fear on the Heaven ladder's final rung.

Whiteness of wave and mountain top are in you, you Mexico harlot and
Hermetic child of tears. And I see the white sand
On your seasoned bed.
Reach bony fingers for the guilt-flung pesos as they
Eclipse the smouldering eyeholes in your head.

King Kong Goes to Saudi-Arabia

While King Konging in Saudi-Arabia
Watched patiently by millions of Saudi-Arabians
Now definitive King Kong monster
To the unravished and mysterious Saudi-Arabian chicks
Of veils and confusing sheets
Who whisper in giggles of King Kong failures in Rotterdam
And points south—

I Grand Prophet and Procrustean Peer of Monsterism
Practise weird voodoo and cabbala magic
Dreaming of a fixed Prime Ministers' Conference
With everyone under my evil spell
Ending in orgy of London streets
Where at last King Kong believed in
By London urchins and fair maids

O England! Home of Monsters!
Of you I dream!
I tell Saudi-Arabian Horrors of your empty coal mines!
I tell them of your tubercular scraggly-haired loudmouthed women!
O England! Guard your dragons!
Feed your vampires!
One day we shall all King Kong thru the streets of Stratford!

A Song of Flowers

Flowers of sadness and of evil
Flowers of the parlours and fields of the dead
Flowers of my Granny dead in a hospital
I do not wonder at your disappearance
Winter is on this land
Laying down endless quilts of quiet sadness
Flowers being good flowers must die in sadness
No flower can be born in sadness
And never ever a flower bloomed in sadness
  lest of course it be a nutty and unserious flower
A flower of the songs of man

Porsche

(for Harvey Glatt)

If I had me a Porsche
A black sleek animal Porsche
I'd find me a brick wall
With two miles of road in front of it
and
    BANG
        me and the Porsche would swing out

For Jenny Louisa Lockyear

"Duerme, vuela, reposa: Tambien se muere el mar!"
Lorca

You holy and now dead old woman
You who so loved Rupert Brooke
and cried for him
annual tears
speaking softly to me of wars
and the ultimate adagio of death
You who read me Tennyson reluctantly
And James Whitcomb Riley digging every line
You who played with me from your wheelchair
Shooting your great gun
a cane
How bloom Yeats' roses this year, old one?
Can you smell them?

Birth

Tomorrow Child
        you bring
Another explosion of daffodils
To ring your entrance of pain.

And crocuses
        mad at eternity
With the promise of fleeting Spring.

Of these flowers I can say nothing;
But of you Tomorrow Child
I can say you will resurrect me
Even before I die.

And the flowers
        fragile and lovely as even you
Will one day be smashed beneath your flying feet.

Billy Graham Goes to Tallahassee

Strange man
        with your Heaven-afflicted eyes
burning this night
            thru sinful Tallahassee
Exhorting & pleading & haranguing the multitudes
                                    like a
                            Southern John the Baptist,
Did you see your living Jesus
                    (for he shall rise up from among you)
        walk down the aisle
                    his beard full of salt and crabs
Whispering soft plans for *your* crucifixion?

Woman from Tallahassee

Too bad you are not here with me now
but gone, gone to Tallahassee
    to work in a coal mine

tubercular, scraggly-haired and loving rice.

I dream inside your rotting lungs and know
ultimately why Tallahassee
    and wonder if you will be able to get
the eyebrow and lash replacements there
    needed badly if you continue to fight

the reality of the sun!

O woman! Heat hoarding Cracker! That coal will diamond and
blind you! Thunder will come heralding the end of you and
Tallahassee too while under the crumbling ruins inspired maggots
scheme fantastic new things!

The earth will reverse itself
                three times
        and then come water
        bringing forth you, naked,
        with all ugliness washed away
        and all life too.

A Monster's Travelogue

Concerning King Kong, aspirant Monarch of England, pussy-footing
rogue in Rotterdam & Cabbala Leader in sandy Saudi-Arabia,
as he travels to Tallahassee

BOOM! BOOM! BOOM! BOOM! BOOM! BOOM! BOOM!

Battered & ball-wracked, immense pilgrim snug in his cups of horror,
King Kong with his nowtime fantastic followers:
Saudi-Arabian spiced & dreamy women—
Turtle eggs & weird chants of Cabbala admirers—
Whores from Holland in reluctant tow—
And sad and lonely tuberculosis of England waving a futile Union Jack—
"I arrive like many another before
"Syphilitic on America's shore."

"O Mason-Dixon Line I lie snug below you!
"O bayou hiding places!
"Plans of conquest! The crackers with their ears filled with dirty wisdom!
"Black-skinned memories of Mau Mau!
"Sad gentlemen in wicked wicked Virginia!
"And a final plowhorse of Tallahassee with leather eyes,
"Suspicious of Alabama & Louisiana!"

"Whole political systems based on the words of Uncle Wiggly!
"My childhood monster hero!
"I have come to absorb you!
"Damns that are dams of overflowing milk!
"The ultimate kindness of abolished zoos!
"Texas Texas Texas!
"I tell you Tallahassee the smell of female sweat is sweeter than that
of juniper or magnolia
"And you will never be a New Orleans!"

What He's Waiting For

Always returning
to his original terror,
life, the doing it once more,
breaking bread,
the meaningless gestures,
changing his death,
not the reality of it,
not the inevitability of it
just the motive.

When the lungs dry up,
he says, when the blood stops
flowing, when the hands curl
inward, you enter
into yourself
& start all over again.

He's still waiting.

The Only Flag

Our mornings indict us.
I have seen it in your eyes,
stark as streets swarm
with sterile savages.

I have no one but you
& you none but me—
& Baby the mathematics of it
are frightening.

Let's go back to bed
lie down together
& forget our fears,
hearts pounding
to the rhythm of love
& your flaming hair
our banner
for that brief moment.

November 17, 1963

This day I shall note
as my British day,
for love sleeps with other men
& I am unconcerned.

But mull over my affairs
real & imagined,
a sad piper for a distant
ridiculous Queen,
I court her favours
desiring thighs
instead of titles
& see her ass
on all my imaginary dollar bills.

Put Down

Don't go down to the river, Love,
bad things
happen there
why just yesterday
a man changed

    change comes
    envelops one

even rocks
I hear
change

& if rocks
make it
why not I
for I want that brightest star
& I'll get it
if somebody
doesn't try to stop me

    shut up
    go to sleep
    are you crazy
    or something

Maidanek

My memory is of skulls
charred remains
of possibilities
& accumulated ash.

I cannot explain
what will not be comprehended,
a collective anguish

thousands of shoes
better explain missing feet.

Four Songs of Experience
(I Ching)

1

First toss
& the head is rapped
by its perspective

vision
or comprehension
forced into
a retired brain

Not to stop
believing
in water
or movement without thought

No springs
gush forth
from the much-heralded ground

it seeps
& the abyss
is filled

in time

2

In my own context
I have accomplished
what I could

If the rains come before harvest—
& it is said they might—
I will be absolved

the Elders
are not
in my context

I am indicted
by falling rain

3

After completion
the analysis
of strength
& its locale
& so with weakness

caution
climax necessitated

At the beginning
no winds blew
& things went well

Now the wind howls
(mouth of a deluge!)
papers are blown about
(motherless of Heaven!)
I am much disordered
& cannot sleep

4

Death is unimportant
because imperative

or the imperative
permanently
displayed
becomes meaningless

(fallen) I
maintain
I am the world's host
who falls
also
I will endeavour
to entertain

        I am waiting

Gratefully
I note
our pit is dry.

A New Light

For seeing, a
brightness within,
a luminous centre

for knowing
where to see
where seeing is—

the movement
beyond the darkened window,
beyond the yard
is seized;
it returns knowing all along
that's me, yes,
there I am,
there too.

Letter

I have parted
with reality,
with words as conveyances,
name what I have occult
or hidden

    I hide from it myself
    as it hides from you.

I am aware
of the mess, repressed,
inside your head,

    the conflicts
    reality imposes.

The cards told me
& knowing, I endure

    am almost happy.

Spring Rain

This black life
this conversing with shadows

& what about reality
or economic aspects,
restricting movement,
halting growth
or the children in a room apart
torturing themselves?

are we not mutations
reconciling diverse things?

is not water
a symbol of life
& this life of death?

is not that haze
before my eyes
spring rain?

For David Wiffen

Why tell the man
the tree (it falls!)
is beautiful

    or that the
    sea is a motion
    its breaking a deception
    on the harbour
    a violent elemental manifestation
    of confusion.

Part of the motion
equal in bearing responsibilities,
is the return
you have called breaking—
all motion returning
into itself.

As a melody is not broken it revolves,
becomes itself

    again & again & again

Impressions of a Mythical Being

1

How is it
in this contest of form
you fall on your ass
& yet win all the prizes?

It must be illusion,
your words: am I not man?
the vibrations from your head.

If I am a continual question
you are an endless answer.

2

Anyone knowing more—pass this.
Anyone knowing less—the same.

(Chanting)
    In puja
    mantra Hosan-i-Sabbah
    Hosan-i-Hosan-i-
    Sabbah-old man-
    mountain-pleasure-
    retaining those
    who would amputate-
    in time-open doors-
    the music out-the foliage-
    flowers-trellis me-
    in time-Horror guru-
    cannabis sativa
    numquam perit-
    sweet scent in head-
    last illusions-

the myth of self-in-time—
in puja
mantra Hosan-i-Sabbah!

3

What are the forms,
the repetitions, at night,
the mandala in sleep in motion,
the becoming that ends with
dawn?

illusion?

Always the question,
hammering, until the rhythms fail
& stop
unanswered.

Grasping it,
having to embrace it,
also the stupidity it registers
left in my hands, damp:
what to do
with preconceptions?
& then the stunning beauty
as the world's green skirts
drift past

& I sleep
but am not
unaware.

4

Real as a rhythm, a notion of power,
now a windowpane you are
light shines thru,
then a morass of pity.

  The song
  quick to lips
  the cry of
  roses
  taunted
  by their thorns

& the change
is in the knowledge
in the need
to change
in the alternative
to change

  the death
  of dust
  where no
  stirring winds
  blow.

5

that I might return, ahead
to the beginning,
as the back of the garden continues
into the front,

note the changes
eternity has made,

made over
not by time
but timelessness,

& flowers
are still dying,

& the turtle
is still on his back,

& I am
is still doubtful.

Youth

laughs against the April rain,
where nothing ages
nor grows old with grace

here, where age
is covered
with illusions.

Here is no wisdom
just the rain,
the rain falling
& mingling
with unshed tears.

The Wall

I'm up against the wall,
up to the coarseness,
surrounded by it.

I have imagined the wall,
am responsible—

you'd think
it is reasonable
to assume
I know what it's for,
but I don't.

I'm painting the wall
green & blue
predominate,
figures shimmer elusive
& I name them.

I'm up against the wall,
I'm part of it
almost, in it
almost, a figure shimmering;
but I don't belong, I don't fit,
for it but not of it
I'll stick around
to see what happens.

Schoenberg

Long-drawn, long tone out-
side my ear, extended regret
bubbles up &
out & down
& in. The song
lonely, the cry
real as the
mechanism conveying it.

Truth is a convenience
few of us
can afford—
the music is really
everywhere cornering
the day's quota of lies
& will soon be working on tomorrow's.

The Seed

There, lilac
heavy hung,
falls freely where it may
& has eyes for blooming
after becoming.

I too am of
seed, fell,
I did, grew
to blossom.

Far mutated, Father,
but a blooming thing nonetheless.

Pounding on the Front Door, Coming in the Back

The poem is a rhythm, a syncopated
vibration, called up from the mind,
required for some purpose, some meaning.

I've lost the reason
for the rhythm, have discarded
the excuses & meanings as unnecessary.
& the sounds have become subtle,
not announced to me.

I cannot tell you the why,
just the is, the
rhythm there, rhythm
transposed, or torn out from,
if you must have meaning,
from melodies, the heart of,
too sad to sing.

Mysteriensonaten

(for Maestro)

To do the beautiful
thing, without hesitating,
is best confined to art.

More so to anticipate
your destruction
in art
& never life.

The firecracker
in a world of bombs
waiting for the right moment.

Fragment of a Conversation
(for Elizabeth)

The same refrain, the
continuances as we sit
& analyse our defeats, noticing how
they oppose one another.

Perhaps we both
shall receive a seedling
letter, instructions on Hope,
from a becoming missionary
of the ideal world.

But we have nourished
intellect on truth
& now it is reluctant
to accept substitutes.

Louis Riel

Preface

I wish to acknowledge as source for the historical data, *Louis Riel* by Brig. George F.G. Stanley. Any divergencies from his strict historical account are of my own unconscious invention.

William Hawkins
Ottawa, October, 1964

"What I most need to do is record experiences, not in the order in which they took place—for that is history—but in the order in which they first became significant to me."

Lawrence Durrell,
Justine

Prologue

But they enter,
he said,
differently—
sceptical
& know, somehow, what they will see
or what they will choose to see;
love even.

Sure, I said,
but I enter dancing,
innocent of that life
& not fearing Know.

& I care
I do
I care.

PART ONE

What I had wanted
have wanted
since the beginning
                was to speak
from where I am
to where you are
Louis Riel

        the prayer then
        being that you
        would be there too
        with me
not under grass, in Deadtown, disgraced—
nor drained of meaning by Time—
nor translated into some other world, not open to me—

        but here, here!
        before me
        where I could know you
        call your name

& talk of that
your Destiny
when we arrived at that one place.

What if he had known
or intuited
standing over Scott's body
the discharge of four guns only
making that death slight to sound
with the sun shining bright
& the "superior" *anglais* blood flowing

that that event
would lead him to 1885 death
& more for him: disgrace
even a mother could not alleviate.

Or of Schultz thought long
who escaped him & roused
Toronto the Good
against his Métis
April 6, 1869

& wished for him dead
instead of simple Scott.

Of him Macdonald said:
"If we get him here
"he is a gone coon."

& Macdonald, that man of biblical verbs,
often praised & revered & dear father called,
seemed not to comprehend the Red River business,
was not aware of what went on;
had no name to call it.

On that same day, April 6,
Abbé Ritchot & his companions,
negotiators for the Settlement
& therefore Riel,
arrived in St. Cloud, Minnesota,
& took trains & other means not known to me
heading for Ottawa.

Who did not know
but must have feared
that they would be arrested in Ottawa
with bleak Toronto warrants
charging them with Scott's murder
much to the satisfaction of the Orange.

That they did fear arrest
or at least hindrance
their different routes
(Ritchot via Buffalo
& Judge Black via Detroit)
surely shows.

& after their release
talks &
the priest, Ritchot, being firm
& Sir John infirm,
he, Macdonald, chucked the whole to Cartier
& went on a bender.

Cartier gave assurances
but no papers
& the same from Young
had Ritchot worried
but not enough.

& Schultz spread rumours,
rumours of Scott buried alive,
the blood running from his true chest,
firing Protestant Ontario with plans of revenge.

A piece of rope
Scott's hands supposedly bound with for his execution
was sent from Schultz to Denison

> who told the latter to show it at meetings
> & suggest there that Riel be hung with it
> their victory assumed over him
> & his death sure
> therefore.

Of the military operation rumours
Ritchot learned nothing,
but Macdonald, it is known, wished Her Majesty's Imperial Forces
& not Canadian troops
to give show of strength on the Red River,
thus intimidating Riel they hoped—

as surely they would.

But Her Majesty's Government
was inclined to let Macdonald stir his own brew,
& keep it from boiling over
with Her but prepared
to eat of it.

But what of his mind,
the thoughts in it when finally aware
that Ritchot had not known Toronto
& its influence
& that Cartier's hands were tied
even on promises
& that death *could* come before the amnesty.

The Bishop Tâché
on his own hook
travelled east to obtain in writing
what Ritchot had by mouth.
No wonder indecision...
troops coming without pardon,
Tâché not heard from...

& so flight
then the horses wandering off
the lost shoe
cold cold cold
all minor compared to bitterness of possible,
maybe apparent, defeat

tho he mumbled about the Manitoba Act accomplishment
& that he considered his work finished

still he went to his mother.

In the Settlement
Goulet dies
drowned—hit on the head with a rock

escaping bloodthirsty Canadians
he sank...

& others:

François Guillemette, beaten to death;
Bob O'Lone, the same;
André Nault, beaten & left for dead;
even Father Kavanaugh, not man of Riel, nearly done in.

All in the name of Scott.

Provincial elections—him out—fear of Orangemen the
reason—fear for family & province's peace also a consideration.

Ending in illness
near to death
seeing Angels

While O'Donaghue plotted
with Fenians
his comical conquest plans.

In 1871 Sir John sent Bishop Tâché $1,000 to be paid Riel over a twelve month period so that he would be able to leave the country & Smith added $600 to that. So that Macdonald could say to the electorate: "Where is Riel? I wish I could lay my hands on him."

PART TWO

"Poetry and History, it seems, must always be a little at variance."
Victor Hugo,
Notre Dame de Paris

Ah my good Louis
good for yet another day
& I am still with you—

with you
& your insanity—
in Ottawa
    a fine place for insanity—
tho I have said nothing of that
it will come

    & of your love speak
    if the spirit moves me
    & of your associates & enemies
    & their actions more must I say.

& that he stood down
in Provencher
    for Cartier
asking nothing for himself
but expecting that mythical amnesty
& good treatment for his people

    & Cartier
    before even assuming office
    up & dies
    & Louis elected again.

He went to Ottawa
& with hip moves
signed in
as Member of Parliament.

Ottawa aghast.

Orange Lodge attendance swells.

Louis Riel! Louis Riel!

But did not sit in Commons

& Schultz
that bastard again
had him expelled.

While Lepine

that great giant
gets nabbed for murder

Scott again
that much murdered man.

& with Lepine

Nault, whom they had tried to kill before
& Lagimodière—

Scott's ghost
working hard.

Louis during this time
at odds with the cosmos

first signs.

That amnesty
when it came
of a bastard sort

banishing him
freeing Nault
& the others
from the noose

the straw that finally broke him.

I call witness to his Washington, D.C. visions:
God in a cloud, he like Moses, only humble, more humble than,

he imagines.

His duties outlined,
his instructions received,

like those of his mother
God telling her to marry
that first Louis Riel, the father,
noble man.

& he then as trilogy
as history:

the Count of Chambord
Don Carlos of Spain
& himself.

March 6, 1876,
yclept by others Louis R. David,
which he denied promptly—

he knew his name
was not to be denied that as well—

admitted
warm with terror
to the Hospital St. Jean de Dieu.

(Manitoba followers
did they know
were they shattered,

& what about mother?)

People in hospital, staff members,
all images to him:

Sister Ste-Thérèse:
"Image of the House of Austria."

Dr. Howard:
"Image of Protestant Russia."

Dr. Lachapelle:
"Image of blackest Liberalism,"
also represents Bismarck
be it noted here.

The hospital then
merely an attempt
to drive the Holy Spirit from him.

Then, because of Orangemen in mind,
taken to Quebec City Funny Farm,

there remaining
until January 23, 1878.

For two years he ran the corridors, naked,
striking mad blows for freedom.

& called himself: Louis David Riel
Prophet, Infallible Pontiff & Priest-King.

& plotted moving the Holy See
from Rome to Montreal.

He did.

What was done to silence his visions
not known

perhaps he just played it cool,
kept them to himself,
waiting for the release
which came

& he dreamed of solitary farms in Nebraska
after it.

PART THREE

"always beware the leader
who talks with God
and leaves you to do the dirty work."
Raymond Souster,
Place of Meeting

Evalina
& me reluctant to deal
with that
as you were even tho far away, Louis,
in Montana.

What can I say here?

That he stayed with her family
& had secret engagement
& he wrote verses
& she excited about his life?

(but where, I say,
could you have gone
little French girl
in what streets wander,
hand-holding, with that man,
Louis Riel?)

but later betrayed
& confused about love therefore
& he married
an illiterate
Métis
& roamed with her
seeking divine buffalo
who knew the various secrets of currency.

Montana
marriage
the return of vision

        & his mission soon to move North-West
        he did not know it
        like Stefansson's
        theory of Empires almost.

Louis all hung up
teaching school
when he *knew* revolt
had schemed impossible victories—

        doomed this event.

In the Spring of 1883
it was
he taught school
& heard the knock on the door

        travelling 700 miles
        Saskatchewan Métis
        need Louis Riel

& in 1884 he took it up again,
he the chosen took his mission
up as he took them
his family up
& he went North-West.

The New Catholic Empire
flashing his brain
& from his brain
& rising up in holy flame
from flat prairie brush.

The Indians meeting too
big councils
throughout the country
all wondering about his mind.

& they in Lorne
not like the Indians their relatives
had no man to say stop
or go

who but Louis Riel
could they turn to?

& so they went to Montana
& God spoke
in whispers now
to him & he came
that agitator, Louis Riel.

& the word
spread
thru the prairies: Louis Riel!

No Orangemen in this tale now.

Now you're a prophet, Louis,
for real
& I am lost, unable to move with you,
with you man of motion of spinning.

You're all wheels Louis,
& find myself going the way of Ritchot
that good man
into stunned silence.

I knew from that first battle
(dead: 12 Horsemen & five of yours)
watching you, unhappy that blood would flow,
holding the cross that helped you prophesy victory,
that in the East 8,000 men volunteered to kill you
& many of your own deserted.

But what of your prayers
do they count for nothing here on my balance sheet
not of judgement
but of knowing
that you could pray for even Macdonald, who said:
"Riel will hang tho every dog in Quebec barks."
& worry about children.

Can I not move
again
from this point
inward
move!
as I have moved before?

To get in close to you
in tight where I could talk as the others did not
to tell you of death
to tell about numbers
about history & heroes.

But what's the use?
your madness
your changing names of the stars
changing the zodiac to rid it of pagan meanings
putting all the priests in South Saskatchewan under surveillance...

That I have failed is now known,
that that earlier part could be justified I never doubted
& that knowledge would be the gap between us...

But Louis in Christ's name for sure
90-year-old men fighting the Mounties
all for your fucked up visions,
lives but glass in your kaleidoscope!

EPILOGUE

Heroes are Destiny's errors
I said to him
fearing Know—

a melodrama
until the real change;
a partnership of
ideal & reality.

& I said
goodbye—Louis, goodbye!

from *Ottawa Poems*

#1

Toward a story, often
a dream in my head, some trip on power
I'm always returning to, towards
a realization of the dilemma,
the pretension of definition

these actual lines of
a life, from it to you
(the forming force)

standing before you
his words for it: the city,
the funny man.

Subject & object
buggering each other.

#2

To Indians
canoeing the Ottawa,
a bleak sight of rock
& tangled shrubs—
a nightmare of growth
clinging to the mountside—

today tourists flock
to peer down

& some
still see Indians
canoeing the Ottawa,
digging the bleak sight of rock
& saying no thanks—

see, they paddle on.

#3

The Funny Kind of Prophet Speaks

Fucking, my dear, you observe
yourself fucking me,
not me fucking you, nor we fucking we.

Or involve yourself with life
through that strange motion
& not so strange rhythm—
like the poems in all our heads, never written,
& that rhythm is past,
present & hopefully the future,
is involved in our creation,
prepares or drains us for death.

When the Heavenly Blitz starts
(the script reads) cities will
explode from the massive rhythm
of us all
trying to get one more in(to)
ourselves, each other.

#4

What had she, Queen Victoria, in mind
naming this place, Ottawa, capital?

Ah coolness, he said,
who dug coolness.

This crazy river-abounding town
where people are quietly
following some hesitant
form of evolution
arranged on television
from Toronto.

where girls are all
possible fucks
in the long dull summernights

& Mounties more image
than reality.

#5

how can I describe the anger
a filled bus overcomes me with
or to, how to justify
hatred of fellow man?

Just one of those
impossible but frequent
happenings...

I want to toughen
my attitudes
on mediocrity

& make a few statements
on values
to the crowded busload.

I reach my stop
& get off—silent
& frightened by visions
of mad house Brockville
& me in real tears, inside.

#6

words the song of birds
insists he, bird words
the song is bird's words—
the words of birds.

outside they sing
(jesus christ I know) words of
the birds, but not of words, not of them,
the words just...

outside they are singing
those bird words.

#7

A Mild Effort at Philosophy

Things disappear fast,
are gone, I'm trying
to replace them as fast
as I can—the plants
in the garden, the no longer familiar
cat, past loves
& even despair.

Generally the past
is more difficult
than the future.

& I don't know
what I can say
about my lack of either.

& the present,
too immense,
provides me one more ending,
but no hint at which way
to begin.

#10

Hey, there, don't
go, a tragedy is shaping
inside my head.

& there's a fire somewhere burning

a man's dreams
I am told
just down the street
burning.

Tragic the death of dreams,
memories of Atlantis,
the symbol, transformed to myth,
lying, used, under the couch,
in Heaven, light streaming from it,
we often don't see.

Some kind of new Viper
is playing drums

as the day finally ends.

#11

Your hair electric, on legs &
traces on breasts, skin tone,
sly ripples of pleasure,
distant explosions
in my ears & always
a burning within
& me lost in my own confusions.

You see I am not inclined
to discretion,
can offer only
obvious love
to all beautiful people—
at night your silence
keeps me awake.

#12

The city extends
no hand to me—
leaves me be.

The frogs I hear are
croaking for something, some meaning,
because I catch their desire.

I am a catcher of desires,
I have been alone
& now love dalliance of the self.

Because of that, the loneliness,
having no one to speak to—
sitting containing
the desire—I send love to all,
screaming it, while the
actual police begin
a pattern of fear
in ever narrowing circles.

#14

Sunday, the small square,
ordered in it, a three-year-old boy,
strangely mine (both resent it)
coaxing some unheard-of melody
from his harmonica.

I, distracted being,
cannot get in tune
but will not let my ego
make judgements
any longer, forced acceptance
of song everywhere
I sing & say
so that's a G harmonica.

& the kid blows a riff
out of his lonely soul, turns me to glass,
me & all my pretensions about meaning.

#15

Ah shit don't shoot I'll sing

I sing:
    Ottawa,
    rivers & jails,
    fantasies
    the dawn can't
    slow up.

I sing:
    for song,
    Ottawa,
    you know nothing
    of poems
    & you are poems.

I sing:
    buses & poison,
    actual criminal exhaust,
    people are falling
    victim to their conveniences

    the man
    vibrated to death
    by an electric toothbrush.

    & me
    don't I take drugs?

Listen Ottawa, I can't sleep

    seem to have forgotten
    the ancient art,

expect too much—
the grey truth of
dawn, now happening,
gives incentives
but it's too late.

Can't you tell me a story?
Get me into one more day?

#16

"Beauty will not wait"*
will not pause
tho I must name it, locate
its area, will not wait
for the namer to compose
himself

as the river
will not, nor
birds on their
particular branches,

nor my memory of China
wait.

You see the sun floods up
forcing the concerns of day
upon me & upon this night
I've spent with old answers
for everyone's new questions—
the rays of light
announce themselves
& simultaneously
the hammering transcription begins,
the unpoetic aspect of breath begins.

* *Charles Olson*

#17

Love, classic form of: to please

ejaculations, how many
did it take to build
the Rideau Canal,
how many Saturday night two dollar bangs?

Listen I'll ask the bus driver
this very morning
how often...

we must have
some norm, some understanding.

Listen, don't feel old
because of love, glibness
or casual fucking is tiresome.

Listen, one day I'm going,
someone will come & take me away.
For smoking shit or pissing on the
War Memorial. For something
they will come & take me.

Who's to say we don't love them
& their cruel ways?

#18

I can't, we don't,
they do.

Grammar lessons
on a river bank
he gives grammar
instead of beauty

knows nothing
about either.

The beauty remains,
they will make it—
only he, strange I,
then unrelated pronoun,
leaves—

see him waving goodbye.

#19

Homage to Batman

Suddenly there were seams
in my mind

I seemed to hear
Batman

feel the acid of his mind.

Remembering forgotten stars,
distant nights,
playing the Joker's crazy & dangerous game...

Something about the failure of past rhythms
driving new tunes out of my head.

#21

Sorry, This is It

You bring me back to the poem,
your movement marks the periphery
I stand upon tonight. Perhaps (counting ways, verbs)

> the sun will change
> the beauty of night flowers
> & the stars I see in you
> will seem less bright then

but this is no concern of mine.

You I am disenchanted that I cannot
speak in symbols about what's
happening, also me not loving
what I cannot touch, a vile man
in vile times, they say of me
"his mind is a mirror dark things groom upon."

> but do not believe Gypsies
> now no word but
> you is in mind.

I is trying to give an apple back
to a laughing Serpent
somewhere in the Near East.

I don't think he'll be back.

#22

You In The Morning

You in the morning,
I wanted to do you totally, more than
ever,

in the evening often I can't
& often I never can as I
would like, to

charge time with love.

Origin of something I have never
carried water in

you confuse me with feelings
I can't name,
can only affirm

& everybody's a Trojan Horse
filled with tender & vicious weapons
& no openings, no
apparent openings.

#23

Hello from the Shadows
(for Christopher Wells)

of the mind & the universe...
the mind, its power is in
the substance of
its object, cosmos, or form—
from without: structure

a time-resisting thing,
contemplating the alley's sacred stone,
my life of ceaseless repetitions,
pointless gestures, initiate
to the magic power of breath,
of symbolic form-structures,

    poor product of nature, acting
    upon what wisdom I have,

I say hello from the shadows
to you, passing on the street.

#25

The Last Train to Narcissus

1

the thing measured, you did, our thing,
in an eye stare measure, after it was
valued, potential for comprehension
noted, & after we had turned down
the noise all around,
a gentle goodbye fell

(My lips have formed
words for the thing
which I will relate one day
in song).

Follow feeling inside,
or the slaughtered moments out, we are
tears falling, we rage...

& these words a response or reaction
to a manifestation within
slowly winding out.

2

the struggle remains unseen,
in the dark, nobody says
much about it

ring yourself round
with roses in the magic
garden, thorns
about the navel to protect,
to cleanse with blood.

Brood on the alternatives
to struggle, weigh the gamble,
the dice may never return, may
forever roll on...

the afternoon falls like passion's
trousers & I illustrate the dark
for you, closing in,

with my knowledge of thorns

adept at instinct
I carry your bags aboard that last foolish train.

#27

Books on Iran Wanted

or conversations with the hip Persian who says
No more prognostications,
people, your *polis* is happening

& it's all therein
this unmentionable

Ten Steps Up or Down

0-	is of course for	(Aleph)
1-	who makes it happen in context	(Beth)
2-	who changes the context	(Gimel)
3-	who cradles my head	(Daleth)
4-	who takes care & reconnoitres	(Heh)
5-	who binds	(Vav)
6-	us as we should be	(Zain)
7-	is power, is consciousness outward	(Cheth)
8-	is power, is consciousness inward	(Teth)
9-	is keeping it hid	(Yod)
10-	is laughing & starting over	(Kaph)

This here is a world of marvels.
Also stern values.

& these moral things, easily acquired,
are hard to use,

spend a whole life
learning when to say
good or bad
at the wrong times

& being as lonely as a poet.

Give this meaning as you may, or must,
at 5:36 a.m. this 6th day of April, year 1966, the sun rose

for me, for you

#28

You there are no more endings, beginning now I won't accept them

(in my dreams women
are mandalas—
four ins & four outs)

You there is a window with light shining thru & shades just
won't stop it

(around me an order
occurs, I feel
it fall back into place)

You now it's quiet & the clock is ticking out of time,
& nothing but vague ideas are suitable, giving form away
I breathe onto glass & direct traffic in the empty street

(you don't know what it is
to have complete control
over nothing)

So I'll write a song
about this boy & a sleigh,
a sleigh & a boy
with no hill
to go down on.

end of the *Ottawa Poems*

The Stupid Saint

Silent as a reversal of life
she loving & cancelling out death considerations
in nocturnal moisture

& dying may wait
until you finish
with this misery, this result
of negative diverse laws
I can never explain
without my hands
on your skin.

Wilful Murder

(for Bruce)

The Saint knows you're a deviate
  & is alarmingly candid about it.
The Saint cannot tip-toe & giggles
  tactlessly while trying.
The Saint plants geraniums & puts down roses
  with a deprecating smile
  & a word about thorns.
The Saint is sure he's right
  & everyone else merely
  intelligently wrong.
The Saint doesn't care about anybody
  except everybody.
The Saint likes himself
  & thinks everybody should
  & he likes them all alphabetically.
The Saint saves his snowballs till July
  hoping for a laugh.

He should get it.

Wystan Hugh Auden

Wystan Hugh Auden
Wrote verse quite sodden.
I knew that he would come to grief
And end up lying for relief.

Wystan Hugh Auden
Was one of the downtrodden
Older boys who persevere
By getting duller every year.

They're the ones who win the prizes
Presenting sheep in multi-guises.
But then if pressed they will confide
Yes, a lion does have pride.

Good bye, good bye, you older boys
Take your rhymes and other toys
So long Auden I'll be like you soon—
Age makes us all our own buffoon.

A Gift for Caesar

As if I could sing up
all we've lost—
you mentioned ten days
& I couldn't understand
a simple span of time.
Not like that,
not just like that.
Recently confusion
marks my every step
& my hands, wanting for nothing,
seldom move.

If you desire
come on here to me,
hand-holding
in a place of no delight,
in flickering fires
that cannot dispel
the cold of night,
we'll remain
yours

Angel of Death in My Dreams

And if existence is only half of existence,
the bad half,
arising hungover & soul
crazy because oh
how his heart
would sing
if he were other than a coward
all the living time.

Funny how
in all the defences we
build, the patterns
we exquisitely form,
none protect us against
the Great Enemy within.
Perhaps the only & lonely
Angel of Death in my dreams

(all seen in the Ides of March
toy-brained Caesar will always reappear
to witness the great triumph
of his death. Et tu, Baby?
his new final sob.)

A Poem About Tomorrow

I do not speak
to make you suddenly silent
as if the distances
between us advertised
the nice guy,
sold as ultimate hog
to hungry millions.

What words fly
in a last offering
to the silent gods!
I have learnt I am a thing,
a sold item
I can't name or even describe.

Some other time
when what is is naught
I'll die whipped out
& famous as a relic
of shrinking promises;
a pet drowned in water,
an animal zoo
charmed by the lines
of manageable movement
in all I love,
in all I'll never be.

A refreshment
taken after midnight;
the concealed listener
whose colour is bad
tunes in the dismal radio
each ethical night.

Before She Could Do It

Before she could do it
she imagined herself do it
to herself

& before she could let me do it
she imagined herself let me do it
to herself

To this day, believe me,
she has never made it
to herself.

A Powerful Cat
(for Mort)

I speak hoping I know where you
think I am.
Disagreement is inevitable
on a mechanical level.
& what is ill-considered
about defence?

On the loose I speak
in passing,
if I'm not here I'm hiding
beyond the mountain of bad karma
I call my gift to the world.

Paper Roses

When a common rose gave up the secret
of blooming & dying:
there should be no alternative
to beauty—
a small part of uncompromised self
to be carried in a pocket
or in a valise
or amulet.

Words are as common as shit
& often equally aromatic.
I like to fling them about
hoping to fertilize
a couple of dozen literate roses
just for you Witches.

The Gift of Space

The hortative
in blank paper
me wife gives

    & I'll have to fill it
    with confetti
    for all the

little Neddies
how they do flit about
those lovely things we had.

This badly made
from scraps of pity;

a world's pulse
within a held breath
& then gasp, the final
lung or needle or whatever
gone to support the great good time
we're not having.

The Warner Mystique

Pause in front of light
as it falls off the bulb
onto us, & marvel.

Thus it is with light
& I would have it be with me,
falling on you
from all possible angles.

Projective Tulips

The Queen of Holland
laid them on us,
all the active colours

as put, ordered,
spaced within sensitive
Canadian mediocre
arrays plurals they are

along a stagnant canal.

To think then they
feel at home, cozy in European jam:
crowd—(big group of diversely
coloured things)

amidst the human debris.

At night the tulip
colour, splashing against the dark,
lights up the love,
the caring of the young

backsides answering
the pulse & flux
of the stars
as they go to it.

Learning lessons
silent flowers only say
& teaching me
yet another way
to see

Expanded Translation of a Half-Remembered Haiku

love is a song tropical fish sing
at my house in the morning.
a song fish sing & we're so
stoned we can't hear it.

no you are not a bad woman,
just a silly one. we are
never so beautiful as when lost
& there are things
we all can see. learn to lose,
the Tao is apparent
& winning simply isn't possible.

The High-Flying Eagle

(for William Roberts)

I know you, Eagle,
have seen you flying about.

What is it you want from me?
Poems? Proof
of conscience?

Fly away now,
I am tired,
my supper is cold
& I can't stand about watching you
always...

Peg's Dream

The house has three floors.
It is a warm
well-lighted house.

On the fourth floor
relatives
(all dead & dusty)
wander amidst huge furnishings;
from the rear of the house
near the stairway
we stand
& listen
as they wail their defeat
at the living.

Autistic

A reordering
or placing of objects in the mind...

one begins choosing
or switching selves
from the ideal to reality

or lying down
in a room
I knew:
        outside
        ladies in girdles
grotesque   ludicrous

men lined up
& applauded
& it appeared...
no, it was
as if a game
were anticipated

I don't know the rules
but I have assurances
from many sources
that it doesn't matter

A Delineation of Memories

(a procrastination for Sheila)

One

Venus I flash & jerk evocative lines as you
move to enter me. Start then the search,
find me lost brother & twin. Lady Sphere
in an avalanche of brothels come to find us,
shopping for love in flesh supermarkets,
mainly unconscious of beauty
as I go along we are.

I'll admit to wondering what has happened
to my dreams, my hopes
for the long ascension, & whatever it means
to be beyond the limit of this scene,
this fatal human context.

You die because you're alive. & always.

Two

In Mars often the disagreeable
guilt afflicts me.

(in my separation
from my lust-mad
family, my horde of dead advisors.)

Who is master of the night, daughter?
My little witch & spawn of lizards—
I now conclude
as a midget in a giant's cave
left with delusions of grandeur
& not even one fantasy outlet
to plug into.

I flirt with my tendencies
& aspire to love.
All my permissions are yours.
I haven't any lies to tell.
I play with instant rules & still lose.

Three

In Jupiter I publish
in defiance of my unpopular profession.

I prophesy death
& smile as you wonder
what I'm trying to invent.

I write about what I get into. I did not invent
death. The concept exists. I can't remember
when I'm lying. Often I simply don't care.
Incest does not frighten me, I am an impossible
brother my sister
if you love me as you do.

He masters his destiny who learns to laugh
through his tears, he who looks long
at the stars
knowing only wisdom produces lasting miracles.
Words are decisions the mind makes,
real self-hood is beyond any decision, Cancer
lady & my friend.

Four

ringed I find you ringed as if to
ring me you would within you
& there's nothing I can do but hope.

Saturn, if resourceful
resolve my tedious affairs—
for we here are ringed in non-matter
& are naked before a universe of incidents.

You are as I call you & what I see
as you fall, or when ascending
a secret place of the gods, not caring
about up or down. A feminine
thing, a hidden thing
suspiciously watery.

I turn light off to on
reaching no conclusions for improved sight.
Seeing less I must
worry more as this day ages. The clock is singing.
The cuckoo is alive with me
but both being unaware
we proceed with caution...
before such cosmic machinery
we seem as cogs to be found within a purpose
not entirely our own.

Five

Uranus my body too keeps a time.
I've studied my own electricity,
have become self-telepathic
in my dualities.

Even though mesmerized by aerodynamics
I grow tired
of unfavourable criticism
by long-dead brethren.

I wish to be free
of tense, alive with the
strength of a moment,
the immediate power
of all temporary things.

The Warlocks of Night don't admit to good or bad.
The Warlocks of Night say we've all been had.

Mr. Gurdjieff won't you please come home?
I volunteer to be used by life,
to continue the long experiment
in relays, if need be.

Six

Neptune, poet, as this house is Muse Manor,
is as myth was,
you dwelled in water
because your ears burned with self-deceptions.

You coach me each time I hide
in the rules of games I'll never play.
Can't you see I'm crazy and useless to designs?

Rumours of diffusion,
a panorama of lies, with things I can't tell anyone of,
and leave me with a conversational capacity
but little to say.

My darling Virgo, avoid carelessness
until I am well again, can think again.

Invocation

When Magus sings the people listen.
His song is often theirs.
Lacking a concept of gender,
he will lead the sexy street
to occupy the song.

Magic is what you know
for sure.

Feel it in my hands
as I try to hold us
& don't know what to say.

Weather Report

As befitting a fool
of such stature
I must scribble
something, show
how alive I am.

Cosmic cannibals
are coming
and they are, they are
going to gobble up all dead things
regardless of previous tradition
or precedent
and I bet they gobble up
half dead things too.

A planet can
evolve beyond a need
for fertilizers.
Death the vomit
of new life laws—

have you noticed how it's getting
colder again?

Stormcentre: Cassandra

Don't worry about enemies
in the middle of this storm.

Hold me tight
We'll go laughing. (Maybe.)

Abyss, abyss, where am I
when you need me?

Walking the line
with Cassandra:
we search each other's eyes for fears
and copulate like demons.

Cassandra's Communication Network

I can't be serious on the telephone
cable of your fears. Fly lady
off that wire.
We'll swirl and die in the open air
and inhabit our dubious destiny
with a grace
communication disallows.

Cassandra on a Bender

So inclined to standards are the traitors
they turn her eyes out from the beauty within.
Hecate, the blossom you gave
this sister's eyes
has withered in the heat of unknown passions.

On the brink
with a drunk
she takes a gulp of red wine,
spilling polka dots on her perfect breasts.

Cassandra's Explicit Sacrament

I call it holy and scoop up my fool's remains
and even that falls from my hands—
sexless Mercury.

I call it holy and cannot approach it
outside of madness—

I'm going away tomorrow.

On His Thirtieth Year

The rain is darkening, heavy;
I have watched it cancel out the garden.
Vision is no more—
I am blind.

I have forgotten
(or I never knew)
the inside and outside of words.
Knowledge is, after all, poignant—

Friends, what does
fucking right off
mean to you?

Bar La Cueva

I live in a heatwave and
my eyes sometimes ache
from this new concept
of hot blue.

They cook
shrimp on cement
in the noon day sun.
Shimmering blue.

At high tide
the ocean is coolest.

"us the sea received."

If you believe this
you'll believe anything.

San Blas, Mexico

Tequila Puro

I'm drunk again. Just a few beers did it
and I'm operating
on yesterday's exhaustion.

Blue again, waiting for
a newscast from California—
it never came.

There is a storm brewing
according to my palm tree
oracular knowledge.
The radio interference
has strengthened my belief.

And over, across the bay,
the lighthouse, the plaintive
horn I sing harmony with.

Of course.

San Blas, Mexico

Another Day in the Bar *La Cueva*

"Screw art. It's an asshole's trade."
Satie

There is a boy,
with intelligent eyes—beautiful with fear.

He can't talk
but aspires to understand.

That's sad.

He sleeps where he falls.

I am fond of silence
and for a few pesos he will smile.

Also he is an epileptic.

San Blas, Mexico

The Ghost of a Rooster Killed by Ritual

Dead—really got it—was launched
into lonely paradise.

I hung little bells about
to keep off demons;
put flowers in the refrigerator.

I worship my electric fan.

During a storm the Rooster's
ghost got blown away. Out, west,
to sea. He's just vapor you know.

Perhaps he be blown all the
way to Japan or India.

They know what to do with ghosts there.

San Blas, Mexico

King Billy, the Disenchanted

"You may my glories and my state depose
But not my griefs; still am I king of those."

as great as grief the nighttime
spirits give way to the sun.

I remember night, remember the moon—
not modest—brightly down
the cobblestone street gleaming
superstitious light.

along such streets we take
the air. No soul stirs
except in certain
peculiar shadows
only we seem aware of
and admit.

Mexico

Recollection of Celebration

So see I for saying saw;
cloudy in mind,
cloudy in fact in day;
even stormy
earlier when exactly
dawn should have—
then was the wind
insistent, ineluctable and strong
in the coco palms.

Flash, I'm trying to learn
chicken talk.
I will celebrate any purpose
fickle or otherwise.

So say anything with your tears
that you see with your eyes
thereby contribute to decreasing lies.

Somewhere in Mexico

October 1st 1968

a catamite
Mexican tenor
singing tartly.

There are three
tributaries
out of Hell.

He knows all three well.

Puerto Vallarta, Mexico

Male/fail Tale

One last poem
for the lady—

she tried
to be perfect in her way.

One last poem
for the gentleman
who made a perfect getaway.

San Blas, Mexico

Mexican Ice Cream Master

"Women are not made
for farewells," he said
as he pissed.

Before dawn he had begun
the process, churning and blending,
plurals of ingredients.

Taste excellence varies
with effort
and his eyes suggest
his is a competitive field.

Sauta, Mexico

Cerveza Superior

Once, Witch said,
she lived by the sea
or that
it lived by her
and there she ate men raw.

I think Witch is
putting me on in this regard.

I have been accused, by
Witch, of course, of being
affected, of being too much
in the vogue, too full
of gutter dishevelment.

I am content to merely hope
her heart stops soon.

San Blas, Mexico

A Walk in A Certain Plaza

An intersection, firstly,
looking into the Plaza,
eyes open, watching for Federales:
none. Looking again for breast and thighs,
trying to work like a zoom
lens. One antique set only.

From the church steeple
the bell becomes rung
and being ringed
by a boy
with awesome rhythmic
precision.

The baleful bastard.

If I had a bell to ring
or another song to sing?

San Blas, Mexico

A Blue Bell

The plaza is a continuation

If I had a bell to ring
or another song to sing.

Yesterday I met
what was acknowledged
as a happy man.

Today
he died
of carbon monoxide poisoning.

He was just grabbing a siesta
in his garage
prone under a running car
with a broken muffler,

at dawn
in a pool of vomit
leaving two empty mescal bottles

his friends say.

Poopsie/Power/Poem

"I am a lie who tells the truth,"
Jean Cocteau

I know nothing of love, there's nothing to know,
You never see it coming, nor see it go.

I held an unconnected
telephone in my hands and tried
to call someone reassuring; the
telephone was blue
and you were naked.

I trembled inside you, five times,
and then ran out into the street
seeking more of the salvation
I just left.

Today I am left with struggle,
trying to create
a new myth for males.

Batting Practice

It has been a long time,
madam, long locked in
space—high, outside,
away from you
kind of thing.

A real throw-away
disposable involvement
we have here.

Two balls,
three strikes—
never swing
on a high outside curve ball.

You're out.

Kearney, Ont.

Forslack and Forless

I ran like water, as river might run,
like, like baby to mother—
Jacob's ladder slowly rung by rung.

I ran over desert, got granular in space,
or, or trapped in an hourglass—
I am not fallen! I jumped from grace.

Fucking Ottawa

Rhyme Suggestion

You bastard!
Sired by a bastard.
Soon whoremaster to become.
How's every little bit
of every part of you
my good old son.

Eggsucker!
Motherfucker!
Cultural swine.
It pains my arse
to be stuck with a farce
like you as a friend of mine.

Kearney, Ont.

When I Fall In Love

I don't even have to try,
try to understand all this.

Deborah, before we arrived it started.
Everything fell right out.

I used to have a pocket I carried love in—
but your music tore a hole in it.

Did you ever swallow a piccolo?
Have elves hid in your hair?

Touching with you was a new feeling.

Toronto

Intimations of Amorality

Hi there, stoned spirit of the flesh.
May I come amongst you?
Would you care to writhe and mesh?

Angel, second order, beloved of god,
To do the boogie is not outlawed.

Magic is what magic does
and that's the truth and it always was.

Kearney, Ont.

The Madman's War

I long to be a carnal scholar!
to essay intimate body details.
I long to speak magic words,
to throw them at some lady's head!

I long to be a war correspondent!
to interview deranged patriots
in some slight nonserious conflict.

If it were credible I would enlist
all the demons Hell hath known
and Frank Sinatra too.

I remain, yours truly,
Zachary Curveball, Lieutenant Commander,
Space Cadets, somewhere
on the North American Front.

The Madman's War: the winter offensive 1973/74

there was a lullaby in the fighting.

I went for a ride in the woods.
I fell off my horse.
I hurt my knee and got violent
with my horse.

My horse ran away and I was still angry.

Casualties were heavy—
I lost my whole fucking army
in the snow.

Currently I am employed as a lumberjack.
Hostilities must cease until
summer warms this old warrior's bones.
Also I am needing a new horse.

A firm steed is what I need.

Declaration of Dependence

I HAVE LOST MY SMALL WAR WITH GOD STOP I WRITE
THIS SO AS TO SUE FOR PEACE STOP KNOWING UNCONDITIONAL
SURRENDER THE ONLY TERMS AVAILABLE STOP I ACCEPT STOP

SEND COLLECT

Suicide Note

feeling old, knowing
it is happening;

beginning to miss that
foolish boy I was upon
a time once.

Getting curious,
perhaps insane, about
the curve, the corner—
around the bend.

My life has had
sordid details;
real associations
with things obvious,
dark and wrong.

Perhaps I do not believe
in God—but I entertained
great expectations.

And hopes, hopes nourished
by many contradictions.

Somebody has been cutting
the quality of life.

Anonymous

O Carole

O Carole, Chuck Berry
should have met you,
with yr short hair,
hard eyes & small
soft & suspicious breasts.

O Carole, when did the
milk of human kindness
go sour & yr lips turn
sneeringly down
bitter with loss?

O Carole, the train is leaving the
station full of sensual blacks
chanting choc-o-late!
choc-o-late!

O Carole, keep the faith.
I am the Tooth Fairy's Agent.

Scarlet Woman With Blue Angora Scarf

Well, she knew
how to boogie
and needed a bath.

Although the stars
were right, the Master Therion's
syringe blocked.

And so she waited,
her bright robes fading
& her need to bathe increasing.

In the rocky landscape
of her mind
there is no water,
no greenery
& little hope.

Untitled Fragment

They wonder why he's so cynical,
this man who bottomed out at the pinnacle
of a rather personal success.
You had to give it to him, he tried his best.

He tried for a piece of everything.
He tried to write, he tried to sing.
But it was in the cards: he had to take a fall;
& so he did and later said it didn't hurt at all.

Sacrifice

The blade's sharpness
is clean—on another astral plane
it would have laser potential—
and it seeks soft flesh. An
immaculate incision.

I cannot offer my own skin
to this altar—
and I wonder, dear,
where you are tonight.

How the Dead Prey Upon You

(For Ottawa)

You and yr past, & re-incarnation, of
all things,
giving you mysterious & yet specious
rights of ownership to a long
catalogue of disgraces
& circuitous lies.

Why not refute the past
and struggle into the future?
You won't have to mix—
stay inside, it is all on TV—
edited for family viewing.
And just like heroin
about five percent real.

Small Ankles, Take Two

Somewhere there
is a girl with small ankles
and I know she waits for me.

She will be refined, this lady,
and delicate—
she will speak in tongues
in the language of The Beast.

Within my recycled mind
I hear strange music.
A dirge, a slow march or processional
to mark her arrival.

I seek ecstasy anticipating
that event.

Dim Aspirations

By candlelight he could pass
as handsome, almost young
& certainly ready;
when the moon breaks free,
bouncing off the snow
he smiles
with his eyes & ears only.

Turning Things Around
(For Jody White)

Everything in my life is broken—
not smashed nor pulverized—
merely chipped, parts worn away by attrition.
I walk aimlessly to & fro examining
the fragments.
Just so as tonight,
I know, behind that cloud cover
the moon's capabilities broaden.
And I know that Demon well—
as he is mine,
as I am his.

Switching Lanes

(For Barbara)

is sanity purpose? Or is
it required, Lady,
in your blonde life?

I look upon the Daisies
you bought—they
stand in a vase beside me,
accompanied by a rose.

I am sure those flowers could talk,
could tell us something.

Unfortunately we killed them,
you and I,
for a smile.

Sheila Frances Louise

I keep my divorce papers
with my underwear, top drawer, in fact,
so that each morning while dressing,
I resolve again,
to stop following my prick around.

No offence now...

Sunrise: Villanelle
(for Andries (Maestro) Hamann)

Day break me a day of no regret.
Make slow or stop the flow of fear of years.
Day break me this day for I've not loved yet.

Can't we as boys and girls—just islands—
Have no great griefs in our brains and time.
Day break me a day of no regret.

Gladsad street child wanting to hang loose.
Needing a child of morning to love and lose.
Day break me this day for I've not loved yet.

I say sing our songs till our songs send us down.
Where we can lay and listen—hear new sounds.
Day break me a day of no regret.

And that's jazz, you sweet old mother of mine.
High-rolling son of stone-empty pockets.
Day break me this day for I've not loved yet.

And go, planets! go on and twist about,
Children die. Mothers cry. None know why.
Day break me a day of no regret.
Day break me this day for I've not loved yet.

Some of the poems in this collection are drawn from the following books by William Hawkins, anthologies and periodicals:

Shoot Low Sheriff, They're Riding Shetland Ponies. With Roy MacSkimming. Ottawa: 1964.
Two longer poems: The Seasons of Miss Nicky, by Harry Howith; and Louis Riel, by William Hawkins. Toronto: Patrician Press, 1965.
Hawkins. Ottawa: Nil Press, 1966
Ottawa Poems. Kitchener: Weed/flower Press, 1966.
The Gift of Space. Toronto: New Press, 1970.
The Madman's War. Ottawa: S.A.W. Publications, 1974.
New Wave Canada. Edited by Raymond Souster. Toronto: Contact Press, 1966.
Modern Canadian Verse. Edited by A.J.M. Smith. Toronto: Oxford University Press, 1967.
The Canadian Forum.
above/ground press broadside
ottawater online journal (www.ottawater.com/).

Acknowledgements

I thank Noel Evans, who provided the impetus for this volume, made the initial selection of poems, and prepared the manuscript. I also thank rob mclennan for finding the book a home at Broken Jaw Press.

WH

About the Author

PHOTO: JAMES GARNER

William Hawkins was born in Ottawa. After side trips to the west coast and Mexico, he resides in the capital, pursuing enlightenment or a reasonable alternative thereto. Hawkins has worked as a truck driver, cook, journalist and musician before settling on the taxi profession as a means of preserving integrity and ensuring near-poverty. His poetry has appeared in six previous collections, various anthologies and many public places. He has recorded a CD of his best songs, also titled *Dancing Alone.*

A Selection of Our Titles in Print

cauldron books series

1 *Shadowy Technicians: New Ottawa Poets*. rob mclennan, editor, poetry, 0-921411-71-5
2 *This Day Full of Promise*. Michael Dennis, poetry, 1-896647-48-0
3 *resume drowning*. Jon Paul Fiorentino, poetry, 1-896647-94-4
4 *Groundswell: the best of above/ground press, 1993-2003*. rob mclennan, editor, poetry, 1-55391-012-5
5 *Dancing Alone: Selected Poems*. William Hawkins, poetry, 1-55391-034-6

A Fredericton Alphabet. John Leroux, photos, architecture, 1-896647-77-4
All the Perfect Disguises. Lorri Neilsen Glenn, poetry, 1-55391-010-9
Antimatter. Hugh Hazelton, poetry, 1-896647-98-7
Avoidance Tactics. Sky Gilbert, drama, 1-896647-50-2
Break the Silence. Denise DeMoura, poetry, 1-896647-87-1
Crossroads Cant. Grace, Seabrook, Shafiq, Shin. Joe Blades, editor, poetry, 0-921411-48-0
Cuerpo amado / Beloved Body. Nela Rio; Hugh Hazelton, translator, poetry, 1-896647-81-2
Day of the Dog-tooth Violets. Christina Kilbourne, short fiction, 1-896647-44-8
During Nights That Undress Other Nights / En las noches que desvisten otras noches. Nela Rio; Elizabeth Gamble Miller, translator, poetry, 1-55391-008-7
Garden of the Gods. Dina Desveaux, novel, 1-55391-016-4
Great Lakes logia. Joe Blades, editor, art & writing anthology, 1-896647-70-7
Herbarium of Souls. Vladimir Tasić, short fiction, 0-921411-72-3
Jive Talk: George Fetherling in Interviews and Documents. Joe Blades, ed., 1-896647-54-5
Mangoes on the Maple Tree. Uma Parameswaran, fiction, 1-896647-79-0
Manitoba highway map. rob mclennan, poetry, 0-921411-89-8
Memories of Sandy Point, St George's Bay, Newfoundland. Phyllis Pieroway, social history, 1-55391-029-X
Maiden Voyages. Scott Burke, editor, drama, 1-55391-023-0
Paper Hotel. rob mclennan, poetry, 1-55391-004-4
Peppermint Night. Vanna Tessier, poetry, 1-896647-83-9
Reader Be Thou Also Ready. Robert James, fiction, 1-896647-26-X
Republic of Parts. Stephanie Maricevic, poetry, 1-55391-025-7
Song of the Vulgar Starling. Eric Miller, poetry, 0-921411-93-6
Speaking Through Jagged Rock. Connie Fife, poetry, 0-921411-99-5
Starting from Promise. Lorne Dufour, poetry, 1-55391-026-5
Sunset. Pablo Urbanyi; Hugh Hazelton, translator, fiction, 1-55391-014-1
Sustaining the Gaze / Sosteniendo la mirada / Soutenant le regard. Brian Atkinson, Nela Rio; Elizabeth Gamble Miller, Jill Valery, translators, photo essay, poetry, 1-55391-028-1
Sweet Mother Prophesy. Andrew Titus, fiction, 1-55391-002-8
Tales for an Urban Sky. Alice Major, poetry, 1-896647-11-1
The Longest Winter. Julie Doiron, Ian Roy, photos, short fiction, 0-921411-95-2
The Robbie Burns Revival & Other Stories. Cecilia Kennedy, short fiction, 1-55391-024-9
The Space of Light / El espacio de la luz. Nela Rio; Elizabeth Gamble Miller, editor and translator, short fiction and poetry, 1-55391-020-6
The Sweet Smell of Mother's Milk-Wet Bodice. Uma Parameswaran, fiction, 1-896647-72-3
The Yoko Ono Project. Jean Yoon, drama, 1-55391-001-X
Túnel de proa verde / Tunnel of the Green Prow. Nela Rio; Hugh Hazelton, translator, poetry, 1-896647-10-3
What Was Always Hers. Uma Parameswaran, short fiction, 1-896647-12-X

www.brokenjaw.com hosts our current catalogue, submissions guidelines, manuscript award competitions, booktrade sales representation and distribution information. Directly from us, all individual orders must be prepaid. All Canadian orders must add 7% GST/HST. CCRA Number: 892667403RT0001. Broken Jaw Press Inc., Box 596 Stn A, Fredericton NB E3B 5A6, Canada.